EXAMPLES *from* THIS BOOK

Who'd expect to find maths at a gymkhana?

A lively board game — who'll be the first to escape?

Mental agility with numbers and money is developed.

Activity tests understanding of 'place value' up to 100.

Challenging activity provides practice in addition and subtraction.

Practises real life maths skills.

1

Maths is an essential part of our lives and our environment. We need to be able to use mathematical skills effectively and with confidence – such confidence can only come from understanding.

In Maths 1 a wide range of activities encourages an understanding of numbers and how they 'work'. Learning to be friends with numbers and symbols is one of our major themes. We also stress throughout the importance of estimating, and being able to investigate solutions to practical real life problems. The activities are divided into four main areas.

NUMBER

6 3 4 5 6 8 1
7 3 2 4 2 5
5 8

Central to the understanding of number, is the 'feel' for the size of a number. Seeing how 'place value' works and what happens when you add on another ten or another hundred are vital steps towards a more confident handling of numbers.

These are some of the activities which emphasise handling number:

Number tricks on page 8 draws attention to the way numbers appear on a calculator or digital counter.

Number busters on page 10 gives an opportunity for checking the understanding of number order and for testing the feel for numbers.

Robbers take half on page 26 gives practice in the essential every day skills of doubling and halving.

Time and the Calendar

Being able to read a clock, watch or calendar are basic skills. Estimating time, linking time with everyday events and carrying out investigations involving time are more sophisticated skills which extend this basic understanding.

These are some of the activities which concentrate on time and the calendar:

Late again on page 28 relates time to daily routine. It encourages your child to estimate short periods of time and then to check them.

Murder on the Wopping Express on page 32 puts telling the time in the context of a murder mystery. Visual information has to be interpreted to solve the crime.

A day at the circus on page 36 practises reading a calendar – a real life mathematical skill which is often overlooked.

 **MEASURE** **SHAPE**

Estimating measurements, judging capacity and being able to measure and weigh accurately are all vital everyday skills. In Maths 2 and 3 there are also activities involving graphs and scale.

These are some of the activities which provide practice in measuring:

On the move on page 40 uses a silly story to develop the feel for the size of various objects, and then leads into a practical measuring activity.

Splot Street summer barbecue on page 42 looks at capacity, using litres. The emphasis is on estimating, then checking through accurate measurements.

In daily life, we frequently need to make decisions which involve spatial awareness, from packing for a holiday to designing and making shelves or cupboards.

Making a tangram on page 21 encourages your child to experiment with a collection of shapes which have been around for thousands of years.

HOW THIS BOOK *works*

You can share in the fun of **Success!** If you want, you can do some of the activities with your child. But **Success!** does not depend on you. One of the benefits of the range is to encourage children to enjoy working independently, not just when the grown-ups are around.

YOU

have a special role to play. It's the one that comes naturally to any parent: give all the encouragement you can!

If you can give your child the benefits of more individual attention, there is no need for you to *teach* specific skills. **Success!** does not require specialist knowledge.

WHEN

you're ready to start on this book at home, sit down together and go through it. Talk about the activities and the zany characters and enjoy the often crazy situations. Start one or two activities to get the feel of them.

Then help to choose an activity to be completed and say that you'd like to see it when it's done.

HOW

will you know things are going well? When your child is absorbed, *thinking* about the activity and really *doing* the work, then you'll know that progress is being made. Look at the back of this book for further guidance.

Speed isn't important. Enjoyment and commitment are the telling signs.

WHAT

should your response be? Praise the results – don't criticise. If you think there is a better way of doing something, suggest it as an alternative, not as the only right way.

Make it clear that working at the activities is a good thing which brings praise. Effort does deserve recognition and it *will* bring results. Not least important, it will give confidence and increase enthusiasm for more activities and more learning.

Look out for opportunities to encourage work on other activities but go for short, frequent sessions – don't let it get boring!

Don't forget to *tick* off each completed activity on the *contents* page and share the sense of achievement and pleasure.

Maths 1

I started this book on.........................

Name...

I finished it on ....

Pssst! It may look like a posh book but it's supposed to be written in — so do it!

Editorial and educational consultant

Dr. Roger Merry

ILLUSTRATORS:

Steve Brookes *Matt Burke*
Jack Haynes

Success!
contents

TICK ALL THE PAGES YOU'VE DONE HERE.

NUMBER TRICKS

Here's a number trick. Try it on your friends! Can you make 7 matchsticks into 8?

Tee hee.

What a dirty trick!

Switch on your calculator and press 8. Can you see how the 8 is made?

Now look at the number 0 on your calculator.
Can you make the same shape with used matchsticks?
Draw it here.

How many matchsticks did you use?

Can you make these numbers from matchsticks?

| 1 | 2 | 3 | 4 | 5 |
| 6 | 7 | 8 | 9 | |

Colour in the numbers 1 to 9 on this calculator. The first one has been done for you.

You can write any number this way.
See if you can write any number from 0-100 in 'digital'.

These matches are delicious!

ON

8

Skulk's Special Spider

Spiders usually have 8 legs. But Skulk's special spider is different. How many legs has it got?

Skulk's special spider catches numbers and puts them *in order* into its web.

Where would it put these numbers? Put the numbers into their correct position on the web.

20   30   40   50   90

Where would it put these numbers?

27   43   56   71   84

Can you put the rest of the numbers into the web? Use a pencil, in case you make any mistakes.

9

NUMBER BUSTERS!

Maud and Elsie and their friends are playing Bingo tonight. But, Elsie's cat Ronald has knocked all the boxes over. **Can you help Elsie put the balls in the right boxes before Maud gets back?**

Look at the page opposite. Colour in red the balls which are in the right boxes. Cross out the balls which are in the wrong boxes. The first one has been done for you.

- Colour in the balls in the right boxes.
- Cross out the balls in the wrong boxes.

Some of the balls are still lost. 5 balls are hidden in the room. **Put them in the right boxes.**

TOO MANY TEETH

Try this – it makes adding up mega easy.

Now you can add up the number of 10's. Then add on any numbers that are left over.

Find the pairs of triangles next to each other which add up to 10. Colour them in. We've done 2 for you.

The star grid contains the following numbers:

5

7 · 2 · 8 · 1 · 5 · 4 · 6 · 9 · 1

6 · 4 · 9 · 3 · 7 · 2 · 8

9 · 1 · 6 · 5 · 5 · 6 · 4

1 · 3 · 7 · 4 · 8 · 7 · 3 · 9 · 1

2

Number of 10's = — — —
Numbers left over = —
Total = — — —

NOW YOU TRY

Can you do the same to help Gus and Hatchet?

Gus and Hatchet have hijacked a lorry. They think it contains used £5 notes.

DENT'S AND SMILE LIKE A MILLIONAIRE

I bet there's a million in here, boss!

I think we've made another booboo, boss.

13

Noah is very worried. He has built an Ark for all the animals. The animals are coming in two by two.

These are the animals:

2 giraffes	2 elephants
2 snakes	2 cats
2 dogs	2 pigs
2 cows	2 lions
2 sheep	2 tigers
2 owls	2 mice

0 1 2 3 4 5 6 7 8 9 10 11 12

But some of the animals don't like each other.
The elephants are too big to share.
No one likes the lions or the tigers, but they don't mind each other.
The cats don't like the dogs, but they like everyone else.
The mice don't like the cats, the owls or the snakes.
The giraffes don't like the snakes.
The other animals don't mind where they go.

How can Noah arrange the Ark?

This is a plan of Noah's Ark. There are 4 rooms which can hold 2, 4, 8 and 10 animals.

1 How many animals can he fit in the Ark?

2 How many animals are there?

3 How can he arrange them?
   Write the names of the animals on the Ark.
   One has been done for you.

l End FETE

Gargoyle's slimy green sponges hit the ghouls with an even number of letters in their name. **Which ghouls did he hit? Colour in the right boxes.**

3

skeleton

vampire

werewolf

spook

2 for 5p

GHOUL TRAIN

4

What dreadful ghoul do Skulk and Gargoyle see? **Join up the odd numbers, in order, to find out.**

THE B-TEAM IN THE SKI-RUN

The B-team are having a skiing holiday.

1 A race! I've never done any skiing before..... it looks a long way down!

Nothing to it. I'll be first down.

2 There's a lot of posts in the way. We'll have to move them first.

You have to ski round 4 posts. You score more points for difficult ones. Let's practise!

SKI-RACE

3 I told you we should have moved them.

That's 17 points to me.

4 That's 7 points.

And it was 15 points for the last one. You've scored 22 so far.

5 Ha, ha, no points for snowdrifts.

GLITCH!

6 Right! This is the race. Everybody ready?

I want to go home!

Nothing to it when you're an expert like me!

Ready, steady, GO!

18

This is how the team raced. Who scored the most points and won? **Fill in your answers at the finish line.**

What is the highest number of points **you** could score? Remember you can only go downhill and you must ski round 4 posts. **Fill in your answer at the bottom.**

Join up the 4 numbers.

Start from here.

YOU

START

MYRTLE   FEETMAN   CANNIBAL   MR. U

15   8   17   12

12   7   19   4

11   14   7   10

18   10   5   16

score

FINISH

The winner was

your score

19

SORTING PONIES

1. 100 ponies have to ride past the judge. Number 1 goes first, then all the ponies in order.

2. What pony comes after 79?

3. What pony comes before 57?

The judge has given prizes to the 5 best ponies. They must ride in order past the judge. But they are all in the wrong order. The pony with the smallest number should go first. Then the next number and so on, up to the highest number. **Can you put them in the right order?**

4.

5. They'll be easy to find. Their numbers are next to each other.

3 ponies have run away. **Can you fill in their numbers to help their riders find them?**

3 | | | 4

Making a Tangram

Hey, Mr. Genius, what are tangrams?

Tangrams are a set of shapes.....

..... and you can make all sorts of different pictures from them – numbers, letters, animals and birds, and many more.

Later . . .

Hey, look! I've made a dog!

A spider for the pot!

1 Cut this square up carefully.

2 Cut along the lines to make the shapes for a tangram.

WARNING!
Read the next page before you start cutting.

3 Can you make all the numbers from 0 to 9?

Remember to use all 7 pieces of the tangram each time you make a picture or shape.

To help you get started, this is how to make the number 3:

Can you make a dog like Weedy's?

Can you make a spider for Skulk?

You can make lots of other shapes as well, like these:

a cat

an aeroplane

ESCAPE FROM Dracula's CASTLE

You are trapped in Dracula's castle. Can you escape before Dracula and his evil companions capture you? Look out for these evil characters. They will try to stop you:

Black Fang, Dracula's terrible guard dog

Bad Boris, Dracula's servant

Skorpion, Dracula's favourite pet

Velda Vampire

Count Dracula

INSTRUCTIONS

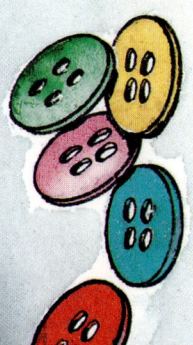

You need:

- a different coloured counter or button for each player
- a dice
- plenty of 2p, 5p and 10p coins — or some paper shapes marked 2p, 5p and 10p — to the value of £6

  Up to 4 people can play

Each player starts with £1. Put the rest of the money on one side. This is the Bank.

You take the money you win from the Bank.

Money you lose goes back to the Bank.

If you run out of money on the way round, you're out of the game.

If you need it, get change from the Bank.

HOW TO PLAY

Take turns to throw the dice and move round the board. **To escape,** you must get round the board and land on 30 at the end. **Keep playing** until everyone has run out of money, been caught by Dracula or escaped. **The winner is the one who escapes with the most money.**

ESCAPE FROM Dracula's CASTLE

ESCAPE COUNT YOUR MONEY

29

The secre... the ca... WIN... You ne... to fir...

You fall into a pit of snakes! LOSE 20p

19

Black Fang leaps out at you! LOSE 30p

21

Bla... Pois... You... W... 2...

17

You find a hidden key! WIN 25p SECRET KEY

15

You blunder into Dracula's Cobweb Trap! LOSE 28p

START

1

Velda Vampire locks you in the dungeon. LOSE 15p

3

You find a hidden passage. Move to Number 13. WIN 32p

27

COUNT DRACULA ATTACKS YOU!

YOU ARE OUT

Give all your money to the first person to escape!

25

...g eats the ...hocolate ...him!

23

Velda Vampire is asleep. Creep past and WIN 12P

Boris drops his knife! WIN 18P

11

Bad Boris ties you up! LOSE 10P

9

5

Skorpion slides down the back of your neck! LOSE 25P

7

You tread on Skorpion! WIN 22P

PUT MONEY HERE

BANK

25

LATE AGAIN

1 Weedy Weasel is always late. 'Breakfast in 3 minutes,' calls his mother. Weedy is still in bed. He jumps out and pulls on his pants, jeans, tee-shirt, sweater, socks and trainers. **Do *you* think he'll be ready in 3 minutes?**

2 'Hurry up, you'll be late for school,' says Weedy's mum. 'Go and wash your face and hands — properly, with soap. Then brush your hair. You've got to leave in 2 minutes.' **Do *you* think he can do it in 2 minutes?**

Can you dress in three minutes in clothes nearly the same as Weedy's?

You can add some things that *you* do at home. Like, how long does it take you to get from home to school?

A Can you guess how long it took Weedy each time? Write each guess for 1 to 4 in the box.

1	Weedy getting dressed
2	Weedy washing his face and hands
3	Weedy eating crisps and drinking tea
4	Weedy watching ads and cleaning teeth
5	
6	

3

Later . . . 'Coming swimming?' asks Sid Genius. 'I'm eating these crisps and having a cup of tea first,' says Weedy. 'But we've got to leave in 10 minutes,' says Sid. **Do *you* think they can leave in 10 minutes?**

4

That evening . . . 'Bed in 5 minutes,' says mum. 'And don't forget to clean your teeth and get a glass of water first.' 'I want to watch the ads first,' he grumbles. **Do *you* think Weedy can watch the ads and still get to bed on time?**

B **Then test your own time, doing the same things as Weedy.** You'll need a clock or a watch.

Look carefully at the time you start and at the time you finish.

Write your answers here.

Guess (in minutes)	Test time (in minutes)

29

MURDER ON THE WOPPING EXPRESS

The man's been murdered. Quick, Rani.... fetch the guard.

I enjoyed that. Let's get back to the carriage. We'll be in Great Wopping in an hour and a half.

Maud has jotted down some questions in her notebook. **Can you help her to fill in the answers and find the murderer!**

1 What time did the train leave Little Wopping?
2 What time did Rani and Sanjay leave the carriage for lunch?
3 What time did the countess come in for lunch?
4 How long did Rani and Sanjay stay in the restaurant car?
5 What time was the train due to arrive at Great Wopping?
6 How long is the train journey from Little Wopping to Great Wopping?
7 How long was the murdered man alone in the carriage?

The murderer is ....

Clues: 1 ....
       2 ....

On the boating lake

1

Maud and Elsie on their way

These boats are all muddled up.

The boatman has 25 boats.
5 of the boats are on the lake.

2

Can you help the boatman?
Put the numbers on the boats, in the right order. Which boats are still on the lake?
Put the numbers on the 5 boats in the circle

A DAY at the CIRCUS

1. Next month the circus is coming to town. I'll take you all. I'll find out what afternoons it's on and when we can all go.

2. Afternoon shows every Wednesday and Saturday for the whole month.

GRUNDLE'S CIRCUS

EVERY WEDNESDAY AND SATURDAY AFTERNOON THIS MONTH!

CALENDAR

SUN		6	13	20	27
MON		7	14	21	28
TUE	1	8	15	22	29
WED	2	9	16	23	30
THUR	3	10	17	24	31
FRI	4	11	18	25	
SAT	5	12	19	26	

3. The circus? I'd love to go. But on the 9th I go to the dentist and on the 19th I'm going to a party.

4. The circus? Great. But every Monday and Saturday I play football.

5. You can count me in. But I'll be on holiday from Tuesday the 15th until Thursday the 24th.

6. ..... choir practice every Friday and on the first Wednesday I visit my Gran.

7. Never mind! I've circled every day the circus is on. Now I'll cross off every day someone is busy ......

Can you do the same on the calendar?

8. Got it! I'll get 5 tickets for

Can you fill in the answer for Lisa?

Ghoul End POST OFFICE

1 The clerk weighs Gargoyle's parcels. He writes the correct postage on each parcel. The heavier the parcel, the more it costs.

How much does the heaviest parcel cost?

How much does the lightest parcel cost?

How much will all 4 parcels cost?

76p 60p 46p 36p

POST EARLY FOR CHRISTMAS

LAST POSTING DATES:
PARCELS: 15 DECEMBE[R]
CARDS:
FIRST CLASS: 21 DECEMBE[R]
SECOND CLASS: 18 DECEMBE[R]

17 DEC

4 Will Gargoyle's parcels reach his friends in time for Christmas?

How many days are left for posting 1st class cards?

How many days are left for posting 2nd class cards?

5 Harry Bonecrusher wants to buy a new television licence. His old television licence runs out on 1st January.

How many weeks and days are left before he needs the new television licence?

DECEMBER				
SUN	1	8	15	22	29
MON	2	9	16	23	30
TUE	3	10	17	24	31
WED	4	11	18	25	JAN 1
THU	5	12	19	26	2
FRI	6	13	20	27	3
SAT	7	14	21	28	4

☐ weeks ☐ days

2 The clerk gave Gargoyle these stamps. **How much do they add up to?**

2 × 50p

3 × 26p

1 × 20p

5 × 5p

£ ____

3 Which stamps should Gargoyle put on each parcel to make the correct amounts? **Write the amounts here. We've done the first one for you.**

76p — 1 × 50p, 1 × 26p

60p

46p

36p

Does Gargoyle have any stamps left? ____

TV LICENCES

6 Skulk has 15 Christmas cards to send. The clerk gives him this book of stamps.

POSTAGE STAMPS

13p × 15
5p × 6
1p × 5
Total value £2.30

How many cards could he send 1st class at 18p each?

Then, how many cards could he send 2nd class at 13p each?

Write your answer here: 1st class ____

2nd class ____

It's easier with a calculator.

On the Move

1

Gus and Hatchet have stolen lots of things. They're moving them into this house.

2

But they've forgotten it's their own house! They're trying to break in through the back window.

3

Hey, boss, it's only 60 centimetres high and 45 centimetres wide!

45 cm

60 cm

4

73 cm

CHOCS

39 cm

56 cm

120 cm

35 cm

30 cm

55 cm

75 cm

68 cm

100 cm

Which stolen goods can they get through the window? Put a tick or a cross here.

Dustbin .... ☐   Stuffed shark .... ☐

Painting .... ☐   Chocolates .... ☐

Tailor's dummy ..... ☐

Can you think of any silly things in your house which Gus and Hatchet might like?

Make a list of silly things here. Measure each one and write down the height and the width in centimetres.

Silly things	Height	Width	✓/x

If Gus and Hatchet stole your silly things, would they be able to get them through their window?

PUT YOUR TICKS OR CROSSES HERE

The police have arrived. **Is Gus too fat to get through the window?**

Help!

We often use *litres* to measure with. Is there a litre measuring jug in your kitchen? Or a bottle marked 1 litre?

Can you find 5 containers like these in your kitchen? Guess how much each holds. Write your guess in the first column.

Use your litre jug or bottle to **measure** how much each holds. Write your measure in the second column.

Bucket

Large Saucepan

Medium Saucepan

Washing Up Bowl

Small Saucepan

Write the names of your 5 containers here.

	How many litres?	
	Guess	Measure
1.		
2.		
3.		
4.		
5.		

Now, can you help Paul, Weedy and Tricia find a good container for their fruit cup?

One of these holds just over 8 litres. We'll use that.

One litre of fruit cup will fill 4 of these tall glasses. There are 30 thirsty children. How many children can have 2 glasses?

a

b — 5 LITRES

c

d

Can you guess which one holds 8 litres? Put a circle around the right letter.

43

AT THE LEISURE CENTRE

The B Team are going swimming at their local leisure centre.

1

I'll pay for all of us. Here's £3.

That's 55p each.

Morning Session

9.30 a.m. – 10.15 a.m.

How much change does Mr. U get? ⬚

2

I can swim 3 lengths.

The pool's 25 metres long.

I can swim 40 metres!

Do you know how far 3 lengths is?

It is ⬚ metres.

Could Mr. U swim 2 lengths?

Yes ☐ or No ☐

3

I'd better try the beginners' pool. It's only 12 metres long.

How long is 3 lengths of the beginners' pool? ⬚ metres

Could Mr. U swim 3 lengths of the beginners' pool? Yes ☐ or No ☐

4

We've paid. You've got to stay in for the whole morning session.

But that's ages. I've got cramp. My foot will drop off!

How many minutes has Feetman been in the pool? ⬚

How many more minutes is it until the end of the morning session?

⬚

44

5 No, no, no! Swim in the 3 lanes with even numbers.

| 1 | 2 | 3 | 4 | 5 | 6 |

Which lanes do they swim in?

Lanes ☐ ☐ and ☐

6 SHOWER

| 1 | 2 | 3 | 4 | 5 | 6 |

The star swimmers are practising a relay race. There are 24 swimmers. How many will swim in each lane? ☐

Later ....

7 We've got £3.30. What shall we have?

Just a drink for me. I don't eat junk food.

REFRESHMENT

CRISPS 16p

CHEWING GUM 15p

BISCUITS 20p INSERT MONEY

NESSY'S CHOCOLATE 22p

WOLFS. GLACIER FRUITS 32p

PEANUTS 25p

HOT & COLD DRINKS 10p

TEA COFFEE MILK COLA

INSERT 10p COIN

Can you help the B team choose something to eat and drink without spending more than £3.30? Make a list and check what it will cost.

ANSWER PAGE

Number busters
Page 10

15, 38, 43 don't belong in 17-36 but 33 does
24, 65 don't belong in 37-53 but 48 does
26, 51 don't belong in 54-68 but 59 does
54, 85, 97, 99, 100 don't belong in 69-81 but 72 does
46, 69, 74 don't belong in 82-100 but 89 does

Too many teeth
Page 12

Number of 10s   = 16
Numbers left over = 8
Total   = 168

Gus and Hatchet have
90 sets of teeth

Noah's Ark
Page 14

This would be a good
place to keep the cats,
owls and snakes,
away from the mice.
The pigs, the cows
and the sheep can go
into either 8 or 10.

Ghoul End Fete
Page 16

Tombola: Gargoyle 43, 67; Skulk 33, 61
Ducks : 28, 30, 34
Stocks: skeleton, werewolf

The ski run
Page 18

Feetman wins.

Best score is 68

Myrtle	Feetman	Cannibal	Mr U
46	49	47	43

Sorting ponies
Page 20

(2) 80 (3) 56
(4) 29, 57, 65, 83, 92
(5) 32, 33, 34

Making a tangram
Page 21

Robbers take half
Page 26

Robbers steal 32, 16, 8, 4, 2, 1
They pay back 2, 4, 8, 16, 32, 64

Skulk gets it wrong
Page 30

Mouldy Rolls 4 extra
Stuffed Rat Pies 8 extra
Fizzy Nightshade 6 extra
Slug and Lettuce 7 extra
Squashed Fly cakes 3 extra
Strawberry and Maggot 5 extra
Bogwater and cream 2 extra

Murder on the Wopping Express
Page 32

(1) 11.30 a.m.
(2) 12.29   (3) 1.10 p.m.   (4) An hour
(5) 3.00 p.m.   (6) $3\frac{1}{2}$ hours   (7) 20 minutes

The bald man is the murderer.
Clues   1. He dropped his glasses in
               the compartment
         2. He's reading the spy book which
               belonged to the murdered man

On the boating lake
Page 34

(2) 9, 12, 15, 23 and 24 are still on the lake
(3) 20p change
(5) Maud and Elsie are 20 minutes late
which could cost £1 extra
(6) They get 40p back, as a reward

A day at the circus
Page 36

Lisa buys tickets for 30th

Ghoul End Post Office
Page 38

(1) Heaviest parcel costs 76p
Lightest parcel costs 36p
The total cost for the parcels is £2.18

(2) Stamps add up to £2.23

(3) 60p 1×50p   46p 1×26p   36p 1×26p
         2×5p   1×20p   2×5p

Gargoyle has one 5p stamp left
(4) Gargoyle's parcels will not get there in time
4 days left for posting first class
1 day left for posting second class
(5) Harry Bonecrusher needs a new television
licence in 2 weeks 1 day
(6) Skulk can send 7 cards first class
and 8 cards second class

On the move
Page 40

Gus and Hatchet can get
everything through the
window except the dustbin.

Splot Street summer barbecue
Page 42

(1) They need 2 big bottles
(5) c
(6) 2 children

At the leisure centre
Page 44

(1) 80p change
(2) 3 lengths is 75 metres
    Mr U cannot swim 2 lengths
(3) 3 lengths of beginner's pool is 36 metres
    Mr U could swim that
(4) Feetman has been in for 20 minutes
    There are 25 minutes left
(5) Lanes 2, 4 and 6
(6) 4 swimmers per lane

the SUCCESS! AWARDS CEREMONY

And now – ladies and gentlemen. The success awards ceremony!

Be the judge and give these famous awards to the pages you thought were best. Write in the names of the activities you choose on the lines.

I give the CANNIBAL GREASY CHIPS AWARD to the activity I enjoyed most.

This was ....

I give the MAUD CRASH HELMET AWARD to the activity I did best.

This was ....

I give the HATCHET STUFFED SHARK AWARD to the activity I thought was the funniest.

This was ....

But I give the GARGOYLE SLIMY GREEN SPONGE AWARD to the activity I thought was the worst.

This was ....

I didn't like this one because ....

Try to give a reason. Was it really boring? Was it not funny? Was it too hard?

47

SUCCESS!
means GREAT IDEAS

" The very best educational process lies in a confident partnership between child, parents and teachers. "

Success! gives you the chance to make your contribution as effective as possible. We provide a range of imaginative opportunities for you to select from. They can be combined in different ways to achieve the progress you are looking for.

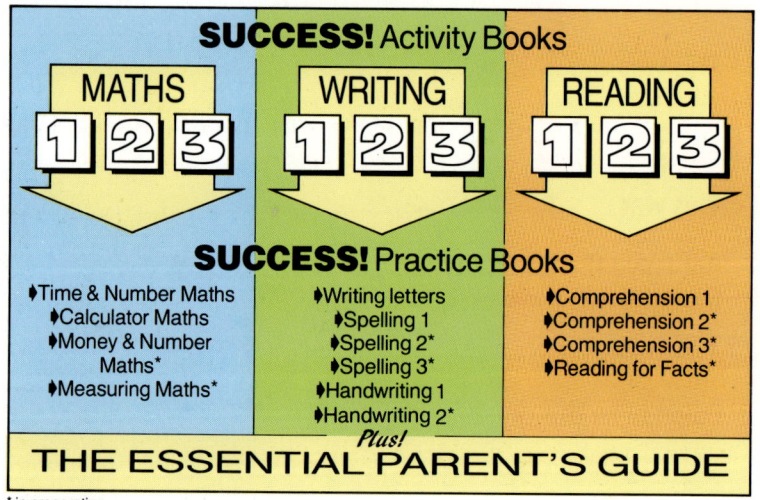

SUCCESS! Activity Books

MATHS	WRITING	READING
1 2 3	1 2 3	1 2 3

SUCCESS! Practice Books

◆Time & Number Maths	◆Writing letters	◆Comprehension 1
◆Calculator Maths	◆Spelling 1	◆Comprehension 2*
◆Money & Number Maths*	◆Spelling 2*	◆Comprehension 3*
◆Measuring Maths*	◆Spelling 3*	◆Reading for Facts*
	◆Handwriting 1	
	◆Handwriting 2*	

Plus!
THE ESSENTIAL PARENT'S GUIDE

* in preparation

SUCCESS! *activity books*

This book is only one of nine activity books covering Maths, Writing and Reading. These books provide challenging and attractive exercises in the *whole business* of the main subjects.
You can choose the subject or subjects that you think particularly need help, and start with the first Level in each one to see how much progress can be made.

SUCCESS! *practice books*

This is a series of books designed to improve specific skills which are part of the whole business of each subject. The exercises are easier than the Activity Books, but they are still lots of fun to do. They concentrate on building ability and confidence in the basic tools everyone needs to be good at the subjects.